SPORTSPEAK

Never a Dead Moment

by
Jack J. Bainter

ISBN: 978-1-60388-114-2
1-60388-114-X

PREFACE

Many sports announcers are talented in their trade. Yet, some are far from being polished in the broadcasting of sports events. For those of us who remember Howard Cosell, we recall him being precise, articulate, and accurate. His vocabulary was enviable, his enunciation admirable, and his wit fitting to the broadcast. Some people found his style abrasive, but at least he never demeaned me by calling me *babee*.

Television sports announcers seem afraid of dead audio time. Viewers can still follow the sports action without begin babbled at for the sole purpose of adding noise. I imagine that many of the senseless comments heard during sports broadcasts are the result of the need, or perceived need, to spew commentary constantly. Yet, it is the inane statements uttered that give us the opportunity to reflect and chuckle. If humor makes our existence more *cheerful*, this book offers 100 lighthearted laughs to brighten our days.

Herein are 100 sports announcers' comments followed by my reaction. Sports mentioned are predominantly basketball and football, but include golf, tennis, baseball, softball, billiards, figure skating, and horse racing.

Enjoy.

SPORTSPEAK

Women's Professional Basketball

1. "Three Mercury players there and neither one could get it."

    Neither of the three!

2. "And a timeout on the floor."

    Where else would there be a timeout?

3. "You can't just guard her with one defender. It takes one and a half."

Oh my, now we are splitting players in half.

Men's Professional Basketball

4. "You can't go wrong with either one of those three."

    Either one of more than two. Oh, oh.

5. "Anytime Rick Smits and Patrick Ewing have been involved in a game, its usually been…"

    Now, it is usually or anytime?

6. "A bunch of second chances there."

   The team had taken four errant shots, but only one was a *second* chance. Then followed third and fourth chances.

7. "The only way you can speculate is after the fact."

   We likely know some politicians who would agree with that.

8. "He didn't guarantee anything, but he did guarantee he would play better."

   Did he or did he not guarantee anything then?

9. "The only way they can make a dent in this series is to outscore the Pacers."

   I agree that outscoring an opponent is required to claim a win, and wins are required to capture a series title.

Men's College Basketball

10. "We'll have two teams at the top of the lead."

    Is it tied for the lead or is it that two teams are not at the bottom of the lead?

11. "He can out-quick anybody." and "He out-quicked his opponent." (Said three times)

    Wow, those guys must have been speedy in those two games.

Jack J. Bainter

12. "The time clock is winding down."

    This is often said near the end of a game, but the time clock starts winding down at the game opening tip-off.

13. "As tight as it can get."

    Marquette was leading by one. Wouldn't a tie score be *as tight as it could get?*

14. "There'll be a little bit of a lengthy discussion."

    I guess a *big bit* would be a mighty long discussion.

15. "They needed that one. They're still down by 18."

    One can't argue with that.

16. "He hung in there and took a percentage shot."

    All shots are percentage shots; some higher or lower than others.

17. "Didn't want to do anything to enhance his recovery."

    Perish the thought.

18. "They want to force the defense to pick up their dribble."

     How is it that the defense is dribbling?

19. "Now Purdue doesn't want to try and get all these points back at once." and "Don't try to get it all back in one or two possessions."

     In both of these instances (two different games) the trailing teams were behind by 13 points. It would be unheard of to make a 13 point play or even 13 points in two possessions.

20. "This is what happens when you let a ball club believe they can beat you."

    Hmm, thought control?

21. "There's no rhyme or reason. They just use them when they think they need to."

    This was in reference to timeouts. It seems to me that a plan to use timeouts when needed at least smacks of sound reasoning.

22. "Boy can he find space where there is no space."

    A little defiance of the laws of physics, I think.

23. "He'll out-effort ya."

    No comment.

24. "This is what college basketball is all about."

> This comment was made with 5.6 seconds on the game clock and Kentucky down by five points. This may be an exciting point in the game, but I suspect college basketball is *about* more than that.

25. "It brings physicality to your team."

> The announcer was referring to having football players on basketball teams. Now we know what physicality means.

26. "They like winning at home."

   And, what team doesn't?

27. "They ended up sitting behind each other."

   This comment referred to how a player had met his future wife. They must have both been contortionists.

28. "A tie ballgame at eight for the fourth time."

> Wow, they just keep tying the game at eight. I wonder what the record is for this eventuality.

29. "You don't wanna be behind going into the last five minutes on the road."

> Just when do you want to be behind?

Jack J. Bainter

30. "All week long, people surmised this game would come down to the end. We're headed that way."

> Every basketball game I have ever seen, or heard of, has come down to the end. Even if a game is cut short, there is still an end.

31. "He's blended this team together."

> Lucky for the team it did not get blended apart.

32. "If they shoot well, we all know what they can do on defense."

   If they don't shoot well, I guess we don't know what they can do on defense.

33. "There's been a lot of conversating going on."

   Yes, this was really said.

34. On numerous occasions, announcers mispronounce lackadaisical as laxidaisical.

    Don't the producers ever listen to these announcers?

College Football

35. "It probably should be seven to nothing."

> Stated at half-time with score 27-7. I suspect the score should have been just what it was.

36. "You got them big linesmen's."

> I can't add anything to that brilliant statement.

37. "Right on the first down marker. He may have it."

    Now folks, if the ball is on the first down marker, the player made the first down. No *may* about it.

38. "They both need that win to get into the best bowl they can get into."

    Hard to argue with that logic.

39. "Penalties are absolutely killing Washington State."

   At the moment of this comment, with nine minutes to play, Washington State, led 21-14 and scored another touchdown two plays later. I guess they weren't really killed.

40. "Grbac couldn't be any better."

   This was in reference to his passing. He was 12 of 15. I really do believe he could have been better with 13, 14, or 15 of 15.

41. "He breaks a tackle."

     Hey, it wasn't a tackle if it was broken.

42. "They needed to play a flawless game today to beat Michigan. They have been less than flawless."

     Decipher that if you can.

43. "They just out-physicaled them."

Poor UCLA, getting out-physicaled by USC.

44. "Tryin' a little trickeration." and "There was a bit of trickeration."

And another new word surfaces.

45. "It's not a loss the coach can really feel good about."

    Just which losses do make a coach feel good?

46. "All of a sudden, the clock keeps running."

    The player was tackled inbounds and rightfully the clock did not stop.

47. "I don't care how much you out-personnel the opponent."

    Mr. Webster, you have our sympathy.

48. "You just can't make a mistake like that."

    They *did* make a mistake like that so I guess they could.

Jack J. Bainter

49. "With all the conjesture about…"

Oops again.

50. "They lost a little something and haven't been able to regain it back."

Does that mean to regain it twice?

51. "If you're gonna beat Purdue this year, you're gonna have to score points."

    I would stake my life on it.

52. "On the exact same play."

    Here we go again with the *exact same*.

53. "He ran north and south for positive yardage."

> Yes, he might have run both directions, but in this case he only ran forward.

54. "They're not taking any precaution here."

> Said about an injured player being removed from the field by cart. What would they have done if they had taken precautions?

55. "One thing that the coach doesn't want is for his quarterbacks to throw interceptions."

Now, I'll bet every viewer believed that to be true.

56. "They had a touchdown taken away from them."

Whoa, it wasn't a touchdown unless it was scored as such. They had what they hoped was a touchdown taken away from them.

Jack J. Bainter

57. "Any time you get into a power game with Michigan State, you are going to lose almost every time."

    Any time or *almost every time.* Which is it?

58. "And he kicks it out of bounds on the other left side of the field." and "Made him throw the ball from his other left arm."

    Oh what fun it must be to play football on a field with two left sides and against a team whose quarterback has two left arms.

59. "Any time the quarterback points, it's usually a run."

    Again, is it *any time* or *usually*?

60. "It's a perfect night for football."

    The temperature was 55 degrees. Who voted that as a perfect temperature? It may be, but there may be those who believe 56 or 54 degrees would be nearer perfect than 55 degrees.

61. "It doesn't matter whether Dittmer gets the ball at the 50 or the 40, he will still have perfect field position."

Ten yards different and both would be perfect. Isn't that remarkable?

Professional Football

62. "What the Bills need is a positive success."

> Now, there's a good idea. Negative success and positive failure are not very rewarding.

63. "Dallas was within inches of scoring the touchdown."

> I suggest that that is the case after every play. It may be 2,000 inches though.

64. "That's as perfect as it gets."

This was said when the field goal kicker was 43 of 44. It just doesn't equal perfect, as good as it is.

65. "It was a forward lateral."

Sorry, if the ball was thrown forward beyond the line of scrimmage, it was a pass and not any sort of lateral.

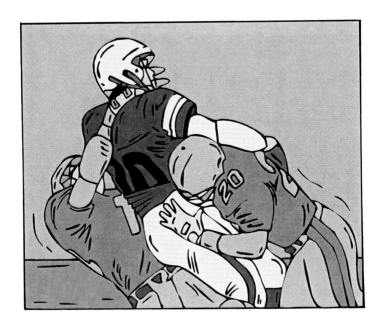

66. "That's just a great football catch."

    What kind of catch did we expect at a football game, a cheerleader catch?

67. "They've got to pick up at least two first downs to have a shot at a field goal."

    Apparently this announcer has never heard of a single first down that went for 20 or more yards.

Jack J. Bainter

68. "This second half is about to get under way again."

    How many starts does it take to get a half under way?

69. "You can't cover a receiver any better than that."

    Bear in mind that the receiver caught the ball and ran for a touchdown. Just maybe he could have been better covered.

Jack J. Bainter

70. "He made a stellar catch by going behind himself."

    Yet another contortionist?

71. "He made a minimal gain."

    The runner made two-and-a-half yards, hardly minimal.

72. "They're a thousand percent correct."

    I'm glad this announcer doesn't do my taxes.

73. "Instead of being in an ideal situation at third and three, it's now third and eight."

    How many coaches think third and three is ideal?

74. "We've got a couple guys watching from up there---right up in the right hand corner."

> This comment referred to astronauts on the moon. But, since the moon is circular, it may be difficult to find the corner.

75. "Fourth and one. Don Shula's gotta make a decision."

> I reckon he made a decision on every play, irrespective of distance remaining for a first down.

76. "He's got some of the longest arms."

    I wonder how many.

77. "It depends on where they mark the ball."

    This comment is heard often in reference to the ball being carried close to the first down marker. But, every down depends on where the ball is marked as to whether it's a first down.

Women's Tennis

78. "Lindsay Davenport doesn't want to lose her serve here."

    Well, just when does she want to lose her serve?

79. "She's playin' to win."

    What an interesting idea of playing to win.

80. "In a long match, I always like the better player, most of the time."

    Once again. Is it *always* or *most of the time?*

81. "Double fault. Bad time for it."

    Just when is a good time to double fault?

Men's Tennis

82. "He didn't have to do that, but he was deep in the air when he hit it."

    I guess that when players are deep in the air, they do what they need to.

83. "Does this window open up here in front of us?" Answer from second announcer: "It does if you have a soldering iron with you."

    This question and answer pertained to the broadcast booth. Even with a soldering iron, it will take a long time to open a window not designed to be opened (and not destroy the window pane). Soldering irons are intended for use in joining metals. Soldering irons are constructive, not destructive, tools.

84. "Agassi has been pouncing on those double faults like prime cuts of beef."

    Aside from an attempt to make a cutesy comment, this statement makes no sense. No player pounces on an opponent's double faults. There is no need to hit the ball to win the point.

85. "Ivan, you've dropped only one set in the whole tournament. How are you playing?"

    I reckon he was playing quite well. What answer did the announcer expect?

86. "You know McEnroe wants it to go to five. Otherwise he has no chance to win."

At this time, play was in the fourth set with McEnroe behind two sets to one. Since they were playing to win best of five sets, it is quite logical that if one needs three sets to win and his opponent already has two sets while he only has one set after three sets of play, he needs two more. Bingo, that would equal five sets.

Baseball

87. "We couldn't be more even."

First, the score is either even or not. Second, it was tied at 0-0, so it was obvious to most fans that the score was even.

88. "You're gonna get hits off him, but you gotta make contact."

Fancy that; needing contact to hit the ball.

89. "If you miss inside, miss at the hitter."

Don't you suppose it would be difficult to miss at the hitter if you missed outside?

Figure Skating

90. "He's had two wins and both were the single most important wins he could have had."

> Maybe this announcer is practicing verbal contortionism. How could two wins both be the single most important?

Softball

91. "Coach Murphy has broughten this program…"

Perhaps it is more significant to have *broughten* something that to have simply *brought* it.

Billiards

92. "He doesn't wanta scratch."

What an absurd bit of commentary. No billiards player ever wants to scratch.

Horse Racing

93. "This is not a good injury here."

    Said as racehorse Barbaro pulled up with a bad leg injury. Just when is there a good injury?

Jack J. Bainter

Women's Golf

94. "They don't do anything they know they're not capable of doing."

    Now, that's a good approach to any game.

95. "She doesn't want to drop three shots on this hole."

    And, on what hole does she want to drop three shots?

96. "Couldn't have landed it in a more perfect spot there."

    Now, we all know there is no degree of perfect; something is either perfect or not. Besides, the shot landed about 10 feet from the hole.

97. "This right here is a golf shot."

    On a golf course during a golf tournament? Fancy that.

98. "She just did not hit it."

    The ball stopped six inches short of the hole. How did it get there if she didn't hit it?

99. "I wouldn't be surprised if this putt finds the bottom of the hole, maybe."

    So the announcer wouldn't be surprised, maybe, eh?

100. "We'll be running out of our allotted time here in just a few moments."

They ran out of time seven minutes hence. That's a lot more moments than just a few.